A RIVER JOURNEY

The Ganges

Rob Bowden

WAYLAND

A RIVER JOURNEY

The Amazon	The Ganges
The Mississippi	The Nile
The Rhine	The Yangtze

A River Journey: The Ganges

Copyright © 2003 Wayland
First published in 2003 by Hodder Wayland,
an imprint of Hodder Children's Books.

This paperback edition published by Wayland in 2007,
an imprint of Hachette Children's Books.

Commissioning Editor: Victoria Brooker
Book Editor: Belinda Hollyer
Book consultant: Glyn Williams
Series consultant: Rob Bowden, EASI-Educational Resourcing

Cover Design: Wayland   Book Design: Jane Hawkins
Picture Research: Shelley Noronha, Glass Onion Pictures
Researchers: Simon Milligan & Martin Curtis
Maps: Tony Fleetwood

Series concept by: Environment and Society International – Educational Resourcing

British Library Cataloguing in Publication Data
Bowden, Rob
   Ganges. - (A river journey)
   1. Ganges River (India and Bangladesh) - Juvenile literature
   2. Ganges River (India and Bangladesh) - Geography - Juvenile literature
   I. Title
   915.4'1
   ISBN-10: 0 7502 4038 5
   ISBN-13: 978 0 7502 4038 3

Printed in China

Wayland,
an imprint of Hachette Children's Books
338 Euston Road, London NW1 3BH

The website addresses (URLs) included in this book were valid at the time of going to press. However, because of the nature of the Internet, it is possible that some addresses may have changed, or sites may have changed or closed down since publication. While the authors and Publisher regret any inconvenience this may cause readers, no responsibility for any such changes can be accepted by either the authors or the Publisher.

The maps in this book use a conical projection, and so the indicator for North on the main map is only approximate.

Picture Acknowledgements

Cover Eye Ubiquitous/David Cumming; title page,Still Pictures/Gill Noti; 3 Impact/Charles Coates; 5 Jane Hawkins; 6 Ecoscene/Robert Weight; Hutchinson/Dave Brinicombe; 8 Axiom/Chris Caldecott, inset Associated Press; 9 Axiom/Ian Cumming; 10 Rex/Jerome Hutin; 11 Rex/ Jerome Hutin; 12 Hutchinson/Andrew Hill; 13 Network/Mike Goldwater, inset Dinodia; 14 Indian Tourist Board; 15 left Eye Ubiqitous/David Cumming, right Hutchinson/Dave Brinicombe; 16 Oxford Scientific Films/Kenneth Day, inset Still Pictures/Rachus Chundawat; 17 Trip/R Lal; 18 Eye Ubiquitous/David Cumming; 19 Eye Ubiquitous/David Cumming; bottom Rex Features/ Simon Wellock ; 20 Trip/H Rogers; 22 Trip/Dinodia; 23 Dinodia/Anil A. Dave; inset Axiom/Jim Holmes; 24 Associated Press/John McConnico, inset Impact/Charles Coates; 25 Associated Press/ Amit Bhargava, inset Axiom/ Paul Quayle; 26 Reuters/Popperfoto; 27 Reuters/Jayanta Shaw; 28 Eye Ubiquitous/ David Cumming, bottom Impact/Charles Coates; 30 Dinodia/ RK Makharia; 31 Trip/F Good, bottom Eye Ubiquitous/Bennett Dean; 32 & 33 Suvendu Chatterjee; 34 Associated Press/ Bikas Das; 35 Eye Ubiquitous/David Cumming; 36 & 37 Suvendu Chatterjee, bottom HWPL; 38 Still Pictures/Gil Moti; 39 Science Photo Library; 40 Popperfoto/Rafique Rahman; 41 Still Pictures/Shehzad Noorani; 42 Eye Ubquitous/David Cumming, inset Still Pictures/Gunter Ziesler; 43 Still Pictures/Gil Noti, inset Still Pictures/ Shehzad Noorani; 44 Still Pictures/Jorgen Schytte, inset Impact/Alastair Guild.

Contents

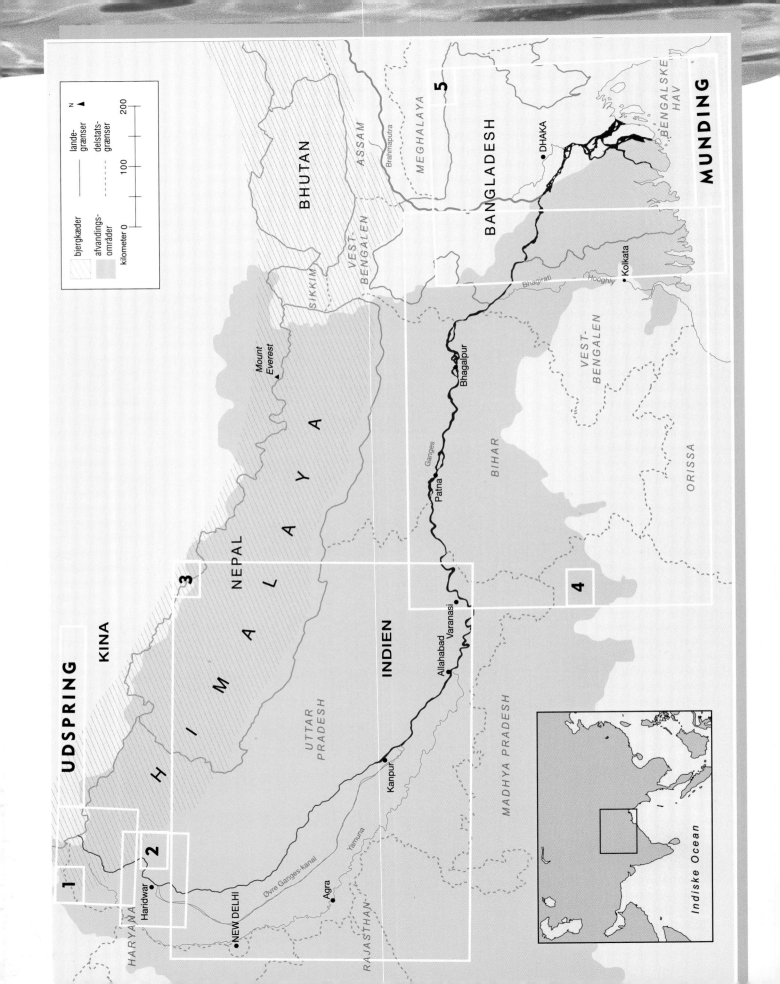

Your Guide to the River

USING THEMED TEXT As you make your journey down the Ganges you will find topic headings about that area of the river. These symbols show what the text is about.

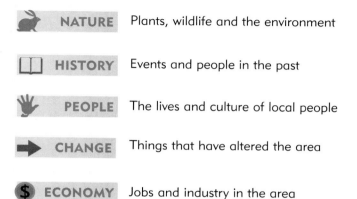

	NATURE	Plants, wildlife and the environment
	HISTORY	Events and people in the past
	PEOPLE	The lives and culture of local people
	CHANGE	Things that have altered the area
	ECONOMY	Jobs and industry in the area

USING MAP REFERENCES Each chapter has a map that shows the section of the river we are visiting. The numbered boxes show exactly where a place of interest is located.

The Journey Ahead

Our journey begins at an ice cave, in the Himalayan mountains of northern India. From here we follow the Ganges as it flows 2,507 kilometres across India and Bangladesh, into the Bay of Bengal.

At first, the river runs through deep valleys and over tumbling rapids. Swollen with meltwater and monsoon rains, the young Ganges slashes through the surrounding rocks, falling ninety per cent of its total descent in the first 500 kilometres.

After Haridwar, the Ganges slows in pace, and we cross a vast plain that supports rich farmland. We explore some of India's major cities, including Kanpur, Varanasi and Kolkata. In Allahabad we watch a spectacular Hindu festival called Kumbh Mela.

We enter Bangladesh across the Farakka Barrage, one of only two dams on the river. The Ganges dominates Bangladesh, and its delta is the largest in the world. The flow of the river - especially in flood - is a matter of life and death for the Bangladeshi people. Then we visit the famous Sundarban wetlands, and end our journey where the Ganges spills into the Indian Ocean.

You'll need your hiking boots! We start our journey with a trek in the mighty Himalayan mountains.

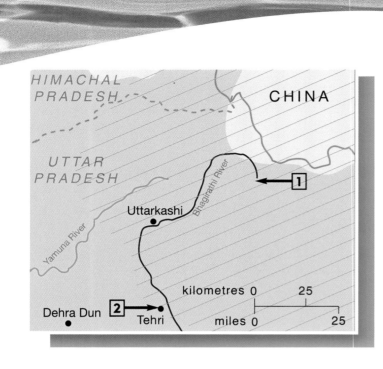

1. The Head Waters

FROM THE FOOT OF THE GANGOTRI glacier, we walk along mountain paths and across fast-flowing streams. Pine forests and snow-capped mountains surround us. Sometimes, scars on the mountainsides mark the devastating impact of landslides and earthquakes. We discover how people survive in this region, and the impact their lives have on the local environment. We also learn a little about the Hindu religion and its close ties to the Ganges River.

Below: Icy waters drain into the Ganges from this glacial landscape, high in the Himalayan mountain range.

Right: This Hindu holy man is called a Sadhu. He has made a pilgrimage to the source of the holy Ganges River, walking on bare feet for hundreds of kilometres.

 NATURE *The Gangotri glacier*

The Gangotri glacier MAP REF: 1 is more than 4,000 metres above sea level. It covers an area of almost 200 square kilometres, and the glacier ice is thought to be at least 400 years old.

The slowly melting ice emerges from a cave in the glacier at the town of Gaumukh. The stream of water, called the Bhagirathi River, becomes the Ganges River later on. Here it dances downstream, carrying chunks of the glacier with it. As we follow its route we pass Hindu pilgrims travelling up to Gaumukh, on foot or by pony. They are coming to visit the source of the sacred Ganges River, which they call the Ganga.

PEOPLE *Holy Ganges*

Of all the world's rivers, the Ganges must have the greatest religious significance. For Hindus, the Ganges is especially sacred, and there are many stories about it. One Hindu myth says that, many years ago, King Sagar had 60,000 sons. The sons, on a quest for their father, disturbed the meditations of a holy man called Kapil Muni. The holy man was so angry at being disturbed that, with one fiery glance, he reduced all but one of the sons to ashes!

King Sagar was beside himself with grief. The gods told him that his sons could only find eternal rest if the goddess Ganga, a river living in the heavens, was brought to Earth. Years later the gods took pity on the unhappy king, and ordered Ganga to fall to earth. Ganga, furious, began roaring and crashing to Earth – but Lord Shiva caught the river in his long, thick hair and tied her up in knots. When Ganga had calmed down, Lord Shiva slowly untied his hair, and Ganga tumbled gently down on to the Himalayan mountain range. Then she flowed across India, washing over the sons' ashes at the edge of the ocean, and freeing their souls as the gods had promised. Ganga's water flowed in seven streams, and one of these is the Bhagirathi River, the one we are now walking beside.

Hinduism is the main religion in India. There are also many Muslims, and there are Buddhists, Christians and Sikhs as well.

Above: Part of the Indian Himalayan mountains.
Right: These children were injured in the
Uttarkashi earthquake in 1991.

 NATURE *On top of the world*

The Himalayan mountains include the highest peaks in the world, and stretch for nearly 3,000 kilometres through Nepal, Bhutan and Tibet. Their stunning peaks, glaciers and valleys also reach into northern Pakistan, Bangladesh and India.

The Uttaranchal region of India, where we are now, includes several of India's highest peaks, such as Nanda Devi and Chaukhamba. Both of these mountains are more than 7,000 metres high.

India and Asia are now joined, but they were once separated by a sea. Over millions of years, enormous pressures beneath the Earth's surface gradually forced the two landmasses to move together. When they finally collided, their edges were pushed up through the sea, and formed the Himalayas.

India and Asia are still pushing against each other, and the Himalayas are still growing! Mount Everest, for example, is already the highest mountain in the world at 8,848 metres. But it is growing up to 2.5 centimetres a year.

Occasionally, the enormous pressure of moving landmasses is released in a sudden jolt on the Earth's surface. This movement is called an earthquake, and it can be a very destructive force. Earthquakes trigger landslides. In populated areas they often destroy buildings, and injure or kill hundreds of people. On 20 October 1991, a massive earthquake struck Uttarkashi near Haridwar. It damaged over 42,000 homes, injuring 5,000 people and killing almost a thousand more.

A staircase of farms

In this part of India, farming provides most families with food and money through subsistence farming. There is a shortage of flat land, and so farmers have developed a clever technique called terraced farming. Small walls are built with rocks, and then covered with earth and grass to hold them together. The walls are built across a slope, and the area behind the walls is filled in with soil to make level terraces.

The terraces provide land for growing crops. They also collect rainwater and reduce soil erosion from the hillsides. Although each terrace is quite small, together they form a giant staircase of farms. You can see cereals, vegetables, pulses and creepers being grown, often all together. This system is called intercropping. Intercropping spreads the work of tending crops throughout the year, and helps prevent a single crop being destroyed by one particular pest or disease.

Below: A 'staircase' of terraced fields climbs up each of these hillsides near Ranikhet.

➡ CHANGE *The Tehri Dam*

In its search for new supplies of electricity for India's growing population, the government has used the power of the Ganges. As water falls it releases energy, and this can be captured and used to generate electricity. Hydroelectric power (HEP) is a clean and renewable form of energy.

In 1961, a site was chosen near the town of Tehri **MAP REF: 2** to build a large dam across the Ganges. The dam is not yet finished, but if it ever is, it will stand 270 metres high, and its reservoir will hold more than 3,000 billion litres of water! When that water is released, the force of its fall will turn giant turbines that generate electricity as they spin. An amazing 2,400 megawatts will be generated, enough to light forty million 60-watt light bulbs.

Although the electricity would benefit India, the building of such a large dam brings problems with it. It is because of these that the Tehri Dam is not yet finished. Supporters of the dam argue that it will provide a cleaner source of energy than fossil fuels such as coal, oil, and gas. The dam will provide thousands of jobs during its construction, and even more through the

Right: Work on the Tehri Dam was started more than thirty years ago, but it may never be finished. Below: This is the Garhwal valley, which will be flooded if the dam is ever completed.

businesses that will be attracted to the area by guaranteed electricity supplies. Water from the dam will provide irrigation for local farms, and the dam itself will help control the Ganges' flow, and protect downstream areas from flooding.

Those against the dam include politicians, environmentalists and scientists. Local villagers are also worried, for 100,000 of them will have to move when the reservoir floods their homes and land. Despite government promises, villagers believe they will not be fully compensated. Scientists point out that the dam is sited in a dangerous earthquake zone. They fear that the dam could burst if there was a big earthquake, like the one that struck Uttarkashi in 1991. If this happened then the holy cities of Rishikesh and Haridwar,

Above: The Tehri Dam reservoir would flood the land and homes of many local people, like this family in the Garhwal valley.

eighty and a hundred kilometres downstream, would flood in less than an hour. Scientists also warn that the dam's turbines could become blocked by sediment carried by the Ganges River. The dam's engineers say this would take 100 years to happen, but others say it might take only thirty years.

During the 1990s, building work on the dam was disrupted by protests. Shri Sunderlal Bahugana, an 81 year-old protestor, refused to eat for 56 days during 1997, until the Indian Prime Minister promised to investigate concerns about the dam. No one knows if the Tehri Dam will ever be finished.

✋ PEOPLE *The Chipko Movement*

In the area around us now, the forest has been cleared to construct roads, or to mine minerals under the forest floor. Forest clearance on this scale is called deforestation. The local population is often blamed for deforestation, because they clear trees to create more farmland, or to use the wood for fuel.

Deforestation is a serious problem in the Himalayas. The trees' leaves work like giant umbrellas and protect the soil from erosion from heavy rains. The roots also reduce erosion, by holding the soil together and absorbing rainwater. Without trees, the heavy rains wash soil down the hillsides and into the river network. When it reaches the Ganges River, the extra sediment slows it down and raises the riverbed. So the amount of water the Ganges can hold is reduced, and the risk of downstream flooding is increased.

Not everyone thinks that deforestation has caused more flooding of the Ganges. Some scientists argue that the deforestation problem in the Himalayas has been exaggerated. They say the people there care for the forest because they use it to provide fuel, food, building materials and medicines. In 1973, one group of local villagers formed a group called the Chipko Movement to protect their forests from logging companies. In Hindi (the second language – after English – of India) Chipko means 'to cling or stick to', and Chipko supporters clung hard to their forests. Some of them actually clung on to the trees, to prevent them being felled.

The Chipko Movement attracted worldwide attention. Their actions led to bans on logging, and changed Indian government policy.

🐇 NATURE *Seasons of the Ganges*

Between November and February the weather is dry and mild. Rainfall is low, and the Ganges flows slowly. By March the air is warming up. Then the snow and glaciers melt, swelling the Ganges and its tributaries. By the end of June, the monsoon season brings warm, moist winds from the Indian Ocean, laden with heavy rains. Monsoon rains often start suddenly, and can last for days at a time.

Left: Sunderlal Bahuguna, one of the leaders of the Chipko Movement. The organisation has been successful in reducing deforestation in the Himalyan foothills.

Many parts of India receive most of their rainfall during monsoon season. For example Lucknow, on the Ganges plains, receives almost eighty per cent of its rain during the monsoon. More rain falls in July, than in all the months from October to June combined. These annual monsoon rains and Himalayan meltwater refresh the Ganges, and bring life to its lands and people.

Above left: Monsoon rains flooding over a path beside the Ganges River.
Above: A landslide has destroyed part of this mountain path. You can see where bushes and trees have been ripped away as well.

🐇 NATURE *Slipping & sliding*

When the material on a slope can no longer be supported against slipping, landslides can happen. Landslides often follow heavy rain, start without warning, and move very quickly. They have occurred naturally for many years in this area, but the risk of future landslides is increased by deforestation and road construction.

In August 1998, heavy monsoon rains caused major landslides in Okhimath, Malpa and Mansuna. Homes, roads, farmland and livestock were washed away or damaged, and nearly three hundred people were killed.

Now we leave the mountain passes, and climb on to a big inflatable raft. Hold on tight as we surge through the narrow gorges ahead!

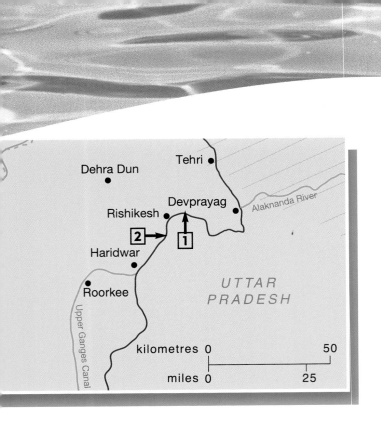

2. The Upper Ganges

FROM OUR RAFT WE HAVE FIRSTHAND experience of the Ganges' power. For fifty-seven kilometres we will fight the rapids and plunge downstream towards the holy town of Rishikesh. We see leopards, monkeys and deer, and visit one of India's most luxurious and environmentally friendly hotels.

When we finally leave the Himalayas at the city of Haridwar, we prepare for a magical journey across the vast Gangetic plain.

Below: Rafting down the Ganges to Haridwar.

Above: The Bhagirathi River meets the Alaknanda River at the hill town of Devprayag.
Above right: These platforms, called ghats, help pilgrims to get down to the river to bathe.
You can see the same ghats in the other photograph, where the two rivers meet.

PEOPLE *Devprayag & pilgrims*

The tiny temple town of Devprayag is 200 kilometres downstream from the Gangotri Glacier. Here, the Bhagirathi River is joined by another river, called the Alaknanda. This confluence is important, because it is here that the river on which we are travelling officially becomes the Ganges.

For Hindus, the confluence of any two rivers is sacred. The meeting of the Bhagirathi River and the Alaknanda River at Devprayag is probably the holiest of them all. The riverbanks are lined with stepped platforms called ghats. Pilgrims gather on the ghats to bathe in the Ganges. They believe the water will wash away their sins, and guide them towards nirvana, which is a state of spiritual freedom. Hindus who live close to the Ganges will often bathe at dawn and dusk, and offer gifts of flowers and food to the river. Holy men, known as sadhus, spend their lives visiting shrines in India, including all the sacred places on the river.

NATURE *Shooting the rapids*

As we journey through the upper reaches of the Ganges, we enjoy one of the wildest whitewater experiences in the world. The river roars deafeningly as it surges around us, swirling through narrow gorges and crashing over rapids. The names of the most spectacular rapids, 'The Fall' and 'The Wall', give a clue as to what lies ahead!

Don't worry though, the river guides are very experienced - they have done the journey many times. It takes just over a week to raft this bit of the Ganges, and we must carry our food, tents, and gear with us. Everything has to go into waterproof bags, to keep it dry in the raft. At night we will camp on sandy banks. These banks form because the river has started to slow down, and deposit sediment.

🐰 NATURE *Rajaji National Park*

Rajaji National Park MAP REF: 1 covers 820 square kilometres. It was created in 1983 to conserve and protect the surrounding environment, and support environmentally friendly tourism.

Rajaji National Park is a nature-lover's paradise. It has up to forty-nine mammal species, 315 bird types, forty-nine fish species and many reptiles and butterflies. Four islands in the Ganges are inside the park's borders, but be careful if you leave the raft to look around. The ducks, herons, and cormorants won't hurt you, but don't get too close to any of the twenty-eight snake species that live here!

As we pass through the park you might see a group of female elephants with their babies, or a tiger picking its way through the long riverside grass. You might even see a leopard relaxing in a tree!

Below: Cormorants are one of many birds that live in the Rajaji National Park.
Right: A group of elephants enjoy a cooling mud bath at the edge of the Ganges

✋ PEOPLE *Threats to the Park*

Rajaji National Park is also home to the Gujjars, a group of migratory pastoral people. They keep herds of buffalo, and move them amongst different grazing lands during the year. Between October and April they stay in the Shivalik Mountains. Then, during the warm, rainy season between May and September, the Gujjars move to the alpine pastures of the Himalayas. As they pass through Rajaji National Park, they use its forest resources for animal feed, fuel wood, housing, and food.

Above: These Gujjar women and child are standing in front of one of their temporary settlements, built from forest resources.

The Gujjars have used this land for centuries, long before the Park was formed. Their traditional use of these resources is important to them. But the park authorities believe that the Gujjars and their herds harm the surrounding environment, and threaten local wildlife. As a result, the authorities are trying to prevent the Gujjars from using the park. If the people who live near the Tehri Dam need to be resettled near the park, that could cause further problems.

💲 ECONOMY *Ganga Banks*

At Ganga Banks MAP REF: 2 we are welcomed to one of the most environmentally friendly hotels in India. Now we can rest after the journey through the rapids! The Ganga Banks resort is set in forests of bamboo and sal trees on the banks of the Ganges. It is constructed of naturally available materials. Not a single tree was cleared to build the resort, and some rooms even have a tree passing right through them!

As tourists become more aware of environmental issues they are prepared to pay more for holidays that protect local environments and their people. This is called eco-tourism. It is becoming a valuable addition to India's tourist industry. As you explore the resort you will see some of its environmentally friendly practices. Wastewater is used to water the lawns, food waste is buried to make compost, and solar energy is used for cooking and heating. Even guests are asked to help by planting a tree when they check in to the resort.

Above: The Har-ki-Pairi ghat at Haridwar
dominates the Ganges River as it flows
through the town.
Right: The river glows softly in reflected light,
as priests float candles on the water.

🖐 PEOPLE *Rishikesh & Haridwar*

We continue by raft to the holy town of
Rishikesh. Nestling on the banks of the
Ganges and surrounded by hills on three
sides, Rishikesh has only around 82,000
people, but it is a centre of meditation and
yoga. (Yoga is a way of exercising that
improves your mental and physical health.)
If all the walking and rafting along the upper
Ganges has exhausted you, then Rishikesh
is the perfect place to relax. There are many
ashrams (spiritual retreats) dotted about the
town.

When we leave Rishikesh we also leave the
Himalayas. Now the Ganges enters flatter
plains. By the time we get to Haridwar, just
twenty-four kilometres downstream, the flow
of the Ganges has slowed down because it is
crossing flat ground.

Haridwar is about three times larger than
Rishikesh. Its name means 'Gateway to the
Gods'. You can see the town bathing ghat -
called 'Har-ki-Pairi' or 'The Footstep of God'
- on the riverbank. The Ganges has a
strong current here, and pilgrims must grip
chains set into the ghat so they don't get
swept away whilst bathing. In the evening
the river takes on a soft glow when priests
offer prayers, and float hundreds of lights
on the water.

📖 HISTORY *The Upper Ganges Canal*

For thousands of years, people living alongside the Ganges River have used its water to irrigate their fields. You can see this very clearly at Haridwar, where a dam diverts much of the Ganges' natural flow into the Upper Ganges Canal. The canal was built between 1842 and 1854 for navigation, and to supply water to over 600,000 hectares of farmland.

At nearly 500 kilometres long, the Upper Ganges Canal was then the largest irrigation system in the world. It is still thought to be one of the world's greatest irrigation works. Engineers marvel at the enormous aqueducts that transport the Ranipur and Pathri rivers over the canal.

Twenty-seven kilometres downstream from Haridwar is the town of Roorkee. Before the canal was built, Roorkee was just a few mud-built houses. The irrigation canal provided farmers with new opportunities to grow and sell food. Now Roorkee is home to more than 150,000 people.

➡ CHANGE *The railway arrives*

Two centuries ago, the Ganges River was navigable all year round. There was even a regular paddle-steamer service between Kolkata and Allahabad that began in 1794. But after the Upper Ganges Canal was built

Above: The Upper Ganges Canal is one of India's engineering triumphs.

navigation on the river became difficult. River transport was reduced, and the paddle-steamers declined when the railways were built in the 1850s.

Railways soon became India's main form of transport. Now there are 62,000 kilometres of track, over 11,000 trains, and 7,000 stations. With a staff of more than 1.6 million, the Indian railway system is one of the largest employers in the world.

Now we can jump on a slow local train, and follow the Ganges River to the ancient city of Varanasi.

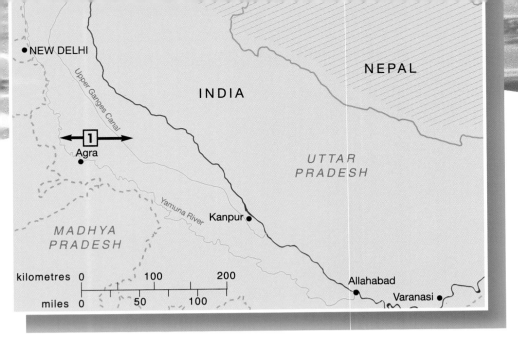

3. The Middle Ganges

WITH THE HIMALAYAS AND HARIDWAR behind us, we enter a very different landscape. The land is some of the most fertile and densely populated in southern Asia. From our train we see a very different farming system to that of the steep valleys upstream. When we get to Kanpur, Allahabad and Varanasi we will leave the train to visit the sights and sounds of these sprawling cities and their fascinating people.

Below: The Gangetic plain between the Ganges and the Yamuna rivers is a great contrast to the mountain headwaters we have left behind.

🐇 NATURE *The Gangetic plains*

Although they are up to sixty-five million years old, the Himalayas are quite young in geological terms. Their relatively soft rocks are easily worn away by heavy monsoon rains. More than 1,000 tonnes are eroded from each square kilometre every year. Much of this eroded rock ends up in the Ganges, and over the millions of years this has been happening, a deep valley between the Himalayas and the Deccan highlands of southern India has been filled in. It is this build-up of mineral-rich sediment that formed the vast Gangetic plain through which we are now travelling.

💲 ECONOMY *Using the doab*

Between the Ganges and the Yamuna rivers is an area of land called the 'doab', MAP REF: 1 which means 'land between rivers'. For many centuries, local people have taken advantage of the annual flooding of the doab, and the rich topsoil this leaves behind when the water subsides.

Above: The fertile soil of the doab is ideal for growing crops such as wheat and barley. Here, the harvest is being dried before it is stored.

The doab soil is further enriched by ploughing in cattle dung and farm refuse, which add nutrients to the soil.

A wide variety of crops can be grown in the doab. In the past, crops were often grown together or in a rotational pattern. Each crop used different nutrients, and so the soil had time to recover between plantings. Although the doab is fertile, water supplies are a problem during the long dry season, when crops such as wheat and barley need watering to prevent them from drying out. The farmers of Auraiya District, through which we are travelling, used to depend on wells, and used buckets to irrigate their crops. The Upper Ganges Canal made large-scale irrigation possible for many doab farmers, and changed farming forever. But an even bigger change was to follow: a change so great, in fact, that it was called a revolution – the Green Revolution.

→ CHANGE *The Green Revolution*

In the mid-twentieth century, India's government was worried about meeting the food needs of its rapidly growing population. In 1966 and 1967 Indian food imports rose sharply following two years of drought, and the government decided to act. They introduced a set of new farming techniques to open up new farmland, and improve production on existing farms. At the centre of this set of techniques were new varieties of staple crops such as wheat and rice, called High Yield Varieties, or HYVs for short.

HYVs were stronger than traditional seeds and had a shorter growing season. This meant that farmers could grow two crops a year instead of one. The first crop was watered by the monsoon rains. The second crop was grown during the dry season, and so farmers had to create an 'artificial monsoon' for it. The answer was a massive investment in irrigation, and the sinking of new wells called 'tubewells'. These are long plastic tubes sunk into the ground, which allow farmers to extract underground water with a motor-driven pump. In 1960 India had just 3,000 tubewells, but by 1990 there were over six million of them, and the area irrigated by tubewells had increased 113 times!

The improvements these techniques brought to Indian farms was so great, it was called the 'Green Revolution'. Although similar measures were introduced in other countries, nowhere was the impact on food supplies so dramatic as in India. Yields of wheat and rice boomed as a result of the Green Revolution. In just ten years, India even had enough of these crops to begin exporting grain. Now, India is one of the world's biggest agricultural producers.

Below: Irrigation, especially from tubewells, has transformed Indian agriculture. Two crops can be grown every year, instead of one.

Above & right: Modern transport equipment and chemicals are essential ingredients of the Green Revolution. Not all farmers can afford them, and chemicals can harm people and the environment.

Not everyone has benefited from the Green Revolution. To succeed, the whole set of measures had to be used – not just the new HYVs but also the irrigation, equipment and chemicals. Many poorer farmers could not afford the expense. Those living in areas of poor quality soil were often ignored by planners, and some farmers who rented good land suddenly found themselves being asked to leave, when landowners tried to 'cash in' on the new opportunities. So many farmers became poorer, some lost their homes, and others went to the cities in search of work.

 NATURE *The Revolution's price*

Although HYV seeds can be more drought-resistant than traditional varieties, they are often more susceptible to attack from diseases or pests, and they require more weeding. Farmers have to use chemical sprays to tackle these problems, but some of these pesticides and herbicides pollute

the local environment and threaten human health by poisoning water supplies or food.

The introduction of HYVs also reduced the traditional varieties of staple crops. Today, for example, India has fifty varieties of rice, but 200 years ago there were an estimated 30,000 traditional species. The missing varieties may now be extinct. This matters, because traditional species may have had better resistance to pests and diseases. They might have reduced the need for chemicals. Now, we will never know.

Above & right: Untreated sewage and dead animals pollute the Ganges River.

 NATURE *The dirty Ganges*

In the city of Kanpur, the banks of the Ganges are lined with leather and textile factories. These industries are very important to the people of Kanpur, but they are also very polluting. Each year they release a staggering 135,000 tonnes of bleach, dye, chemicals - even animal carcasses - into the Ganges.

Pollution on this scale is not limited to Kanpur. Over 200 million tonnes of industrial waste are emptied into the Ganges every day. Chemicals used in farming, and bodies cremated on the riverbanks, add further to this pollution. The biggest cause of pollution is human sewage. More than 1,300 million tonnes are dumped into the river daily. At the same time, people rely on the Ganges for water to wash, cook, and even drink. Pollution in the Ganges makes its water a serious health risk.

 PEOPLE *Pollution & health*

Water pollution and poor living conditions are a major problem for Kanpur's residents. The Ganges provides over half the city's water, but pollution levels are as high as 340,000 times the acceptable levels. People are often exposed to dangerous chemicals, and are often sick.

Diarrhoea is especially common, but cholera and typhoid are also spread by polluted water. These diseases cause fevers, and dehydration, and in severe cases they can kill.

Cholera and typhoid were once common everywhere. Now, clean water supplies and improvements in sanitation have wiped them out in western Europe and North America. In India, however, nearly seventy

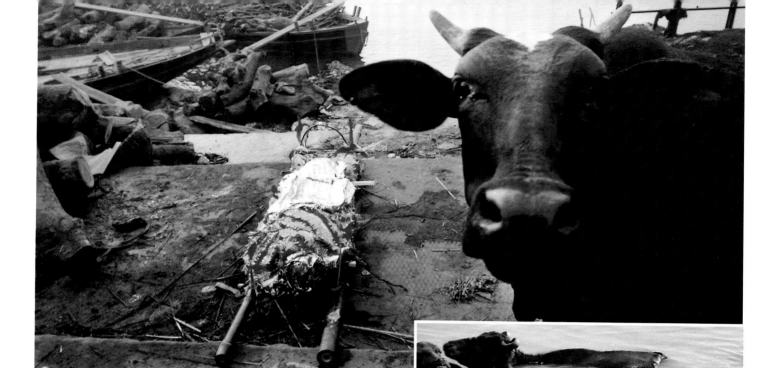

Above: Many Hindus believe that it is especially holy to be cremated on the Ganges River.
Right: Ganges water has many uses - here, a farmer washes his buffalo.

per cent of the available water is polluted, or carries disease. So if you get thirsty, remember to boil, filter or purify the water first.

➡ CHANGE *Ganges Action Plan*

In 1985, the Indian government launched the Ganges Action Plan, which aimed to clean up waste before it entered the river. New sewage-pumping stations were built, and people were educated to better care for the river environment.

But despite spending over US$330 million, the plan has been described as one of India's most dramatic failures. Many projects are incomplete, others do not work properly, and sewage treatment plants don't work at all during the regular power cuts in this part of India. A scheme to encourage the use of electric pyres for cremating the dead has also failed. The authorities apparently ignored the Hindu belief that bodies cremated on the Ganges go straight to heaven.

Since the Ganges Action Plan was introduced in 1985, the amount of sewage flowing into the Ganges has actually doubled. Less than twenty per cent of it is treated to make it safe.

NATURE *The three-way junction*

Almost 200 kilometres downstream from Kanpur, we reach the ancient city of Allahabad. Some people call Allahabad by another name - Tribeni Sangam, which means 'three-way junction'. This is the place where the Ganges meets two other rivers of great religious importance to Hindus: the Yamuna River, and the mythical Saraswati River.

Like the Ganges, the Yamuna River begins life high in the Himalayas. It travels for 1,370 kilometres, flows through India's capital, New Delhi, and past India's most famous building, the Taj Mahal at Agra.

The power of the Yamuna River restores the dwindling flow of the Ganges. The Saraswati River, however, adds nothing physical at all. In fact, the Saraswati only exists in the tales of priests and sadhus, and in the minds of millions of devout Hindus. Geographers have long searched for evidence of this mythical river, but its source and course still remain a mystery.

Below: A satellite image of the confluence of the Ganges (the muddy river) and the Yamuna.

 PEOPLE *Out of this world*

The place where the Saraswati River is believed to meet the Ganges and Yamuna is sacred. This is the holiest place on Earth for a Hindu to bathe. Every twelve years, Hindus gather in enormous numbers to celebrate a 2,000 year old festival called 'Maha Kumbh Mela' - the Great Fair of the Vessel of Immortality. Sadhus and priests meet for prayers, and millions of Hindus bathe in the Ganges' purifying waters.

In January 2001 about thirty million Hindus travelled from around the world to celebrate Maha Kumbh Mela. It was the biggest gathering of people the world has ever seen. The Allahabad authorities built a temporary city with 400,000 tents, 75,000 latrines, and sixty-one access roads. Thousands of tonnes of flour and rice were eaten during the month-long celebrations. Preparations help to make the festival safe, and safety is important. In 1954, 300 people were trampled to death, and in 1989 more than 3,000 people were reported lost, some of whom were never found. In 2001, special camps were set up for lost people, and although 180,000 people were reported lost they were all reunited with their families.

You might be lucky enough to visit Allahabad during the next Maha Kumbh Mela in 2013, but you don't need to travel there to see it! The festival is so enormous, it can be photographed from space.

$ ECONOMY *Tourism in Varanasi*

Varanasi is an ancient centre of trade, education, religion, art and culture. It was settled by the Kasis people over three thousand years ago, and the city's famous silk industry dates back nearly as far. With such an interesting past, Varanasi today attracts visitors from around the world.

We can join some tourists on an early morning boat trip, and watch a centuries-old Varanasi tradition. As the first rays of dawn turn the Ganges a shimmering red and gold, Varanasi's famous ghats fill with people. These Hindu bathers visit one of the hundred or more ghats that line the western bank of the Ganges each morning, to offer 'puja' (worship) to the rising sun. Then we might head into the hustle and bustle of the old city, and search the maze of alleyways for a souvenir of beautiful Varanasi silk.

We take a rickshaw ride across town to our hotel for the night. These three-wheeled vehicles provide transport in most Indian cities. They are powered either by small motor engines, or human pedal power!

At the hotel we have wonderful views of the Ganges from a high terrace. But watch out for the monkeys who love to steal food and cameras - they are the true rulers of Varanasi's rooftops.

Left: Each morning in Varanasi, thousands of Hindus fill the ghats beside the Ganges River and offer prayers to the rising sun.

 PEOPLE *The caste system*

Traditionally, Hindu society is organized into different social groups known as 'castes'. The Brahmans (priests and academics), are the highest caste, followed by the Kshatriyas (rulers and warriors) and the Vaishyas (traders and professionals). The Shudras (skilled workmen, labourers, and servants) are the lowest. Another group of people have an even lower staus than the Shudras. These people are called Dalits, which means 'the oppressed', and they have no caste at all. About fifteen per cent of the Indian population are Dalits.

The caste system is not as strong as it used to be. In India's cities today, different castes work, travel, eat and socialise together. But caste is still important, and it influences many aspects of daily life. For example, some upper castes still believe they will be polluted if they come into contact with Dalits. Marriage between people of different castes is very unusual.

Although all Indians should now be treated equally, Dalits can often find only undesirable jobs, like cleaning toilets or collecting garbage. In rural areas, social divisions are still very strong. There, Dalits may be forbidden to enter Hindu temples, or even prevented from collecting water from certain village wells.

We leave Varanasi by rowboat and head downstream to the city of Patna.

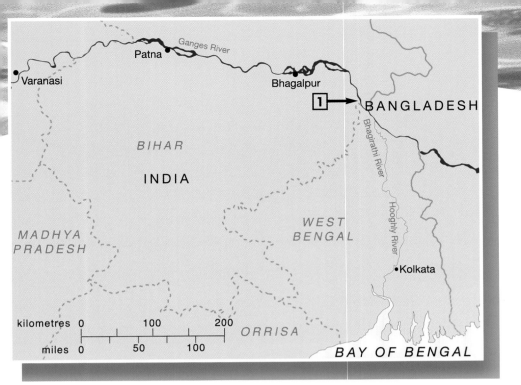

4. The Lower Ganges

Below: The Sikh temple in Patna was built at the birthplace of Guru Govind Singh, the 10th Sikh Guru. It is a significant place of pilgrimage for Sikhs.

THE CITY OF PATNA IS THE CAPITAL of Bihar state. Patna is also an important historical settlement. In the farmland around the city we learn more about rice and its importance to the Indian economy. We search for the Ganges river dolphin, and discover the fascinating process of silk production in the city of Bhagalpur. Then we travel along the Hooghly River to visit Kolkata, the biggest city on our journey.

Above: The Golghar was built as a huge granary, but it has become one of Patna's most unusual tourist attractions.

📖 HISTORY *Patna*

Patna's history dates from the fifth century BC, when it was called Pataliputra. Legend says that King Putraka built the city for his queen, Patali.

Pataliputra was the centre of some of India's earliest kingdoms, but it was deserted by the seventh century AD. Then, in 1541, the city grew up again as Patna. At that time it was ruled by an Afghan King of the Mughal Empire (a Muslim kingdom that once controlled much of South Asia). The British ruled Patna from 1765 until 1947, when India gained independence.

Patna's varied past is all around us. The Sher Shahi Mosque is a famous Muslim landmark, built in 1545. The Sikh shrine of Harmandirji marks the birthplace of the Sikh Guru, Govind Singh, who was born here in 1766. One unusual landmark is a giant granary, known as Golghar. This dome-shaped structure was built by the British in 1786 to store grain, after there was a terrible famine in the region. The granary was never used, but if you climb to the top of the twenty-nine metre structure, you will have fantastic views over the city of Patna and the Ganges River.

💲 ECONOMY *Rice cultivation*

As we leave Patna we travel through vast fields of rice growing on either side of the Ganges. Rice cultivation began in India some 5,000 years ago and it is still one of India's most important crops.

In 2001, India produced 22.5 per cent of the world's rice, and was the second biggest producer of rice after China. Much of India's rice is consumed within India, but one variety, basmati rice, is a very valuable export. India exports around 650,000 tonnes of basmati a year. Around sixty-five per cent of this goes to Saudi Arabia, and the rest to Europe and North America.

Below: Rice is India's most important crop. In many villages along the Ganges, it is still harvested by hand.

NATURE A *freshwater dolphin*

The Ganges river dolphin is a member of the dolphin family, but it looks quite different to ocean-going dolphins. It can grow to two and a half metres long, and is a grey-brown colour. Its long-toothed beak is used to catch fish, squid, crustaceans and even turtles.

Like all dolphins, the Ganges dolphin emits noises that bounce, or echo, off objects. This is called echolocation, and helps the dolphins locate their prey. Echolocation is vital for the survival of Ganges dolphins because they are almost completely blind. Unusually, they swim on their sides and drag one flipper along the river bed. This is another way in which the dolphins navigate and search for food.

The Ganges river dolphin is an endangered species. Dams, irrigation, fishing, industrial pollution and river traffic have all had an impact on them. In 2001, there were only about 4,000 left in the wild.

$ ECONOMY *The Silk City*

Almost 200 kilometres downstream from Patna we reach Bhagalpur. This city is so famous for silk production that is often called the Silk City. Silk is a valuable animal fibre, produced by 'silkworm' caterpillars as a building material for their cocoons.

In Bhagalpur, commercial silk production (called sericulture) still follows traditional processes. First, the silkworm cocoons are collected by hand from wild mulberry bushes,and left to dry in the sun. Next, the cocoons are soaked in a boiling bath. This softens the gum that binds the silk fibres together. Then a skilled worker called a reeler takes individual fibres from several cocoons

Opposite: This young woman is a 'reeler'. Her hands are moving so fast they look blurred in the picture, as she unwinds silk from the cocoons.
Above: The 'charka' loom this woman is using to spin silk has to be turned by hand.
Right: After the silk has been washed and dyed, it is hung up to dry in the sunlight.

at a time and unwinds, or unreels, them to form a single thread of silk. Although each cocoon may be just three centimetres long, the reeling process can produce a single continuous fibre 900 metres long! Finally, the thread is woven into silk fabric.

Bhagalpur workers mainly use handlooms; there are only a few power looms in the city. After further treatments, including washing and dying, the silk is graded, and then sold.

Indian sericulture has grown dramatically since the 1970s. By the mid 1990s, India was the world's second biggest producer, with thirteen per cent of world production. Much of this increase comes from silkworm farms. Only a few places still collect cocoons from the wild, as they do in Bhagalpur.

HISTORY   *The East India Company*

Indian silk was one of many products that attracted British traders to India in the seventeenth century. The East India Company was formed in 1600 by the British government. Its job was to control British trade and interests in the whole region.

The Company concentrated on its valuable trade in India, and that made it wealthy and powerful. Soon the East India Company also took over competing traders. Gradually, it controlled most of the Indian subcontinent. The East India Company even had its own army, with 24,000 soldiers.

In 1784, the British government decided to take direct control of Indian affairs, instead of leaving it to the East India Company. The Company gradually lost its power. It was closed down after the Indian Mutiny of 1857-58. In the Mutiny, Indian soldiers serving in the East India Company mutinied against their British officers.

$ ECONOMY   *Kolkata*

Kolkata (formerly spelled 'Calcutta') is located on a branch of the Ganges called the Hooghly River. The Hooghly is part of the enormous Ganges delta. We follow the Hooghly River on a diversion from our main route to visit Kolkata, the biggest city on the Ganges River system.

It was Kolkata's location that attracted the East India Company to it in 1690. The Hooghly River made Kolkata an ideal trading centre. It provided easy shipping access to both the Indian Ocean and the Ganges River. Indian merchants flocked to the city, and by 1772 it was the capital of British-controlled India.

Trade is still essential to Kolkata's economy. Trade and commerce employ

Below: The first fixed bridge across the Hooghly River was built in 1874, but this second bridge was added in the 1990s. It is called the Vidyasagar Setu, and is a cable-stayed girder bridge.

around forty per cent of the city's workers. One tenth of India's imports, and one twelfth of its exports, pass through Kolkata's ports.

✋ PEOPLE *The Partition of India*

When India gained independence from Britain in 1947, it was partitioned (split) into three countries. The old British India became modern India, Pakistan, and Bangladesh. (Bangladesh was part of Pakistan from 1947 until 1971.)

Partition was based on religious grounds, and it caused an enormous movement of people. Thousands of Hindus moved into India, and thousands of Muslims moved into Pakistan and Bangladesh. Most of the Hindus who left Bangladesh in 1947 settled around Kolkata, just over the border. More Hindus followed after Bangladesh became independent in 1971. The Kolkata region became the most densely populated part of India. In the days of the British Empire, Kolkata was one of India's richest cities. Today it is one of the poorest.

In 2001, Kolkata had a population of 4.6 million people. A further 8.4 million people live in its suburbs. Such huge numbers of people in a city with limited public services means that many live in great poverty. Slum areas, called 'bustees', have no water, sewage or electricity, and almost a quarter of a million people have no housing at all. They live on the streets in a cycle of hardship and despair, with no way out.

A Catholic nun called Mother Teresa got the world's attention for Kolkata's bustees. She won the Nobel Peace Prize in 1979 for her work with the poor of Kolkata, and for her efforts to persuade the Indian government to help them.

Below: Many of Kolkata's poorest residents live in makeshift shelters on the city streets.

➡ CHANGE *The Farakka Barrage*

Now we are back on the Ganges, but our route downstream into Bangladesh is blocked by the Farakka Barrage MAP REF: 1 . This dam was built by the Indian government, to improve navigation around Kolkata.

The Farakka Barrage diverted some of the water from the Ganges River into the Bhagirathi and Hooghly rivers. That increased the flow of water, and helped ships to navigate more easily into Kolkata's ports. The extra water from the Farakka Barrage improved navigation around Kolkata. This, in turn, helped the Indian economy.

✋ PEOPLE *Water disagreements*

As soon as the Farakka Barrage opened in 1976, it was the subject of serious disagreements between India and Bangladesh.

The Bangladesh government feared that the Barrage would prevent enough water reaching their own country. A water shortage in the Ganges River would be disastrous for

the Bangladeshi economy. Estimates showed that water shortages of this kind would cost Bangladesh over US $500 million a year. The impact on agriculture, fishing, industry and navigation would be enormous.

Some experts also believed that if India opened the barrage during periods of high flow, the sudden rush of water would cause widespread flooding and further economic damage.

In 1977 the two countries signed an agreement over India's use of the Farakka Barrage. It stated how much water India could withdraw from the Ganges without harming the economy or people of Bangladesh. This first agreement, however, lasted only five years.

Below: The Farakka Barrage stretches across the background of this photograph. There is a road on top, for traffic to use.

Although further agreements followed, each one was short-lived. It was not until 1996, twenty years after the barrage was opened, that India and Bangladesh signed a lasting Ganges Water Agreement.

The two countries now co-operate to share and manage the Ganges, as well as other rivers in the region. This partnership is vital, because the region's population and demand for water will continue to grow in the future.

We catch a lift with one of the local fishing boats, and head for Bangladesh. This is the final part of our journey.

The map shows:

INDIA

Brahmaputra River

BANGLADESH

Dhaleswari River

Ganges River

DHAKA

INDIA

WEST BENGAL

1

BAY OF BENGAL

kilometres 0   100

miles 0   50

5. The Ganges Delta

NOW WE LEAVE INDIA AND ENTER Bangladesh. The people of Bangladesh depend on the Ganges. In good times they farm its fertile soil, but in times of flood their lives are threatened by its rising waters.

We see where southern Asia's second great river, the Brahmaputra, joins the Ganges. Together, these two rivers form the world's biggest delta. We explore the marshy Sundarban forest, at the southern edge of Bangladesh. And finally, we watch the Ganges River flow into the Bay of Bengal.

Below: A Bangladeshi farmer harvesting jute, one of the country's most important crops.

Right: In this satellite image you can see the Ganges and some of its distributaries flowing across the continent, and into the Bay of Bengal.

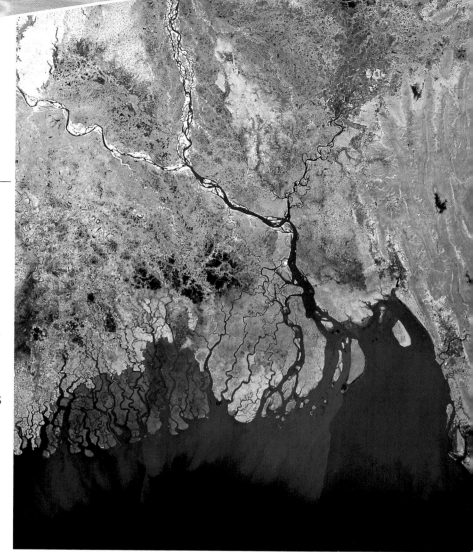

 NATURE *The giant delta*

About 200 kilometres downstream from Farakka, the Ganges is joined by the Jamuna River. The Jamuna is the lower part of the mighty Brahmaputra River. Like the Ganges, the Brahmaputra began life high in the Himalayas.

By the time they meet, the Ganges and the Jamuna have slowed down. They have started to deposit the massive loads of sediment collected on their journeys. Now they are one river, but sediment blocks the main path. The river is forced to split into channels as it finds its way to the ocean. These channels are called distributaries.

The Ganges River has eight main distributaries, and there are hundreds of smaller ones. The entire delta region covers an area of around 75,000 square kilometres, which makes it the biggest in the world.

PEOPLE *Fertile floodplains*

Bangladesh's delta is one of the most populated in the world. Many of the country's 132 million people depend on the delta for their survival. Two-thirds of Bangladeshis work in agriculture, and grow crops on the fertile delta floodplains. Jute fibre, used to make twine and sacking, is Bangladesh's main export crop. Tea, wheat, rice, pulses, sugarcane and fruits are grown for export as well as for local consumption.

Most of Bangladesh's farms depend on the annual flooding of the Ganges to bring fresh supplies of nutrient-rich sediment to their fields. But living in the path of the Ganges is a risky business. One way people have adapted to this risk is to build their homes on top of earthen platforms, or embankments. They hope this will protect them from all but the most severe floods.

NATURE *Monsoon floods*

No matter how carefully the Bangladeshi people prepare for floods, nature is dangerous and unpredictable. An especially long and heavy monsoon season brings disaster. Sometimes the Ganges floods so badly that it covers two-thirds of Bangladesh in water. This causes billions of dollars of damage, and hundreds of deaths. One of the worst floods in recent history was in 1998. Around 1,000 people were killed, and more than thirty million were left homeless by floods. The floods lasted more than two months. The entire rice crop was ruined, and the government asked for almost US $900 million dollars of aid to help it feed and re-house people.

PEOPLE *Dhaka & the poor*

Dhaka is the capital of Bangladesh, and home to more than eight million people. Many of these people are among the poorest in the world. One organisation that tries to help Bangladesh's poor is the Grameen Bank, based in Dhaka.

The Grameen Bank was founded in 1976 to help poor rural Bangladeshis borrow money and start up small businesses.

Below: Peddle-powered rickshaws struggling through one of Bangladesh's floods. Some rickshaws are powered by small motors.

Above: The Grameen Bank has now loaned more than US$1 billion to its members, ninety-four per cent of whom are women.

This simple scheme has transformed the lives of over 2.4 million people. Their former poverty meant that ordinary banks refused to lend them money. Today, the Grameen Bank has expanded into a whole range of enterprises to fight poverty. These include support for village industries, such as weaving and fishing. It also provides services such as telecommunications and the internet.

The Grameen Bank has been so successful that it has been copied. Similar schemes now run in about forty-three other countries, including neighbouring India.

$ ECONOMY *Gas reserves*

One of Bangladesh's best hopes for defeating poverty are its gas reserves. These lie under the delta region, and offshore in the Bay of Bengal. Important discoveries were made during the 1990s, and several major oil companies have invested in gas exploration in Bangladesh.

The most important gas field, the Sangu, is an offshore one. It began production in June 1998. In 1999, Bangladesh produced about 320 billion cubic feet of natural gas. This was used to produce agricultural fertilizers, generate electricity and power vehicles. It is also used for cooking and light. With estimated reserves of between eleven and thirty-three trillion cubic feet, Bangladesh's gas future looks very good.

Above: A riverside village on the edge of the Sundarban forests and swamps.
Left: The Bengal tiger is the most powerful cat on earth. It weighs 180 to 230 kilos and grows up to five metres or more in length.

![rabbit] NATURE *The Sundarbans*

Now we take a small boat to explore the Sundarbans. MAP REF: 1 This vast area of forest and swamp spreads across the fifty-four islands that line the southern edge of the Ganges delta. The dense vegetation around us is one of the last untouched areas of Bangladesh. Very few people live here.

The Sundarbans belong to the wildlife of southern Asia. Threatened species like the estuarine crocodile, the Indian python and the endangered Bengal tiger live here. Interest in Bengal tigers has led to a growing tourist industry. Rich visitors will pay high prices for a glimpse of them. We will be very lucky to spot a tiger, but they can probably spot us - for as the local saying goes, 'Here, the tiger is always watching you!'

The Sundarban area has an important role in protecting Bangladesh from storms. Fierce storms are common here during the monsoon season. The Sundarbans' thick mangrove vegetation acts as a natural barrier. Without it, Bangladesh would experience much greater damage.

Cyclones, called hurricanes or typhoons in other parts of the world, are severe weather systems. They result in a mass of swirling and fast-moving winds and rain. With wind speeds of up to 250 kilometres per hour, cyclones are extremely destructive if they hit land. They are among the world's worst natural disasters. In coastal areas, cyclones are often followed by an equally destructive storm surge, when large waves rush inland at great speed.

The natural barrier of the Sundarbans is no match for a severe cyclone or storm surge. Throughout Bangladesh's history, its people have had to cope with the devastating effects of these tropical storms. In 1970, Bangladesh suffered the world's worst recorded cyclone, when about 500,000 people were killed. The last bad cyclone to strike Bangladesh was in 1991. It killed 139,000 people, and made millions more homeless. Most of the dead were killed by the storm surge, which reached heights of six metres and stretched over fourteen kilometres inland.

After the 1991 cyclone the government built concrete shelters, and introduced an early warning system. The new system seems to work. In 1997, a 200 kilometres an hour cyclone killed fewer than fifty people.

Left: A cyclone shelter, built after the devastation of 1991.
Below: Bangladeshi homes destroyed by a cyclone.

$ ECONOMY *Shrimp & salmon*

We leave the sheltered wilderness of the Sundarbans on board a local fishing boat. Fishing has long played a part in the lives of Bangladeshi people, and its inland fisheries are the third biggest in the world after China and India. Fish is particularly important in Bangladesh. It provides the main source of protein in the diet of many people.

Our boat heads out to where the freshwater of the Ganges mixes with the saltwater of the Indian Ocean. This brackish (slightly salty) water is ideal for producing shrimp by a new and fast-growing type of fish farming called aquaculture. Here, high-value fish like shrimp and salmon are farmed in large containers or cages that are submerged in the open water. The fish are mainly sold for export. In 1998, Bangladeshi aquaculture produced 584,000 tonnes of produce worth almost US$1.5 billion.

Unfortunately, intensive aquaculture can cause disease to spread into wild stocks of fish. Sometimes captive fish escape and endanger local wild species. Many experts describe acquaculture on this scale as an ecological disaster.

Above: Fish drying in the sun on the edge of the Indian Ocean. Drying fish is a cheap way of preserving it.
Right: A fisherman casting his net into the delta. Fish farming, however, is replacing traditional methods of fishing.

➡ CHANGE *Global warming*

The greatest change Bangladesh and its people may face in the coming years will probably be the threat of global warming. This is the gradual warming of the Earth's surface caused when carbon dioxide and other greenhouse gases are released into the atmosphere.

One of the likely results of global warming is a gradual rise in sea levels. This could be 0.5 metres by 2100. That

might not sound very much, but it would mean that six million Bangladeshis lost their homes. It could permanently flood the low-lying delta region we have travelled through. Global warming could also increase the frequency of cyclones, and alter the timing and severity of monsoons.

If warmer temperatures also melt glaciers and snow in the Himalayas, the whole Ganges region will face a much higher risk of flooding. No one knows if global warming will happen this fast. But if it does, the journey we have just made will not be possible in another hundred years.

We have reached the end of our journey - and the end of the Ganges, the holiest river in the world. The people and places of the Ganges River are fascinating in their variety. Now that you have experienced this for yourself, you can follow the area's fortunes in the future.

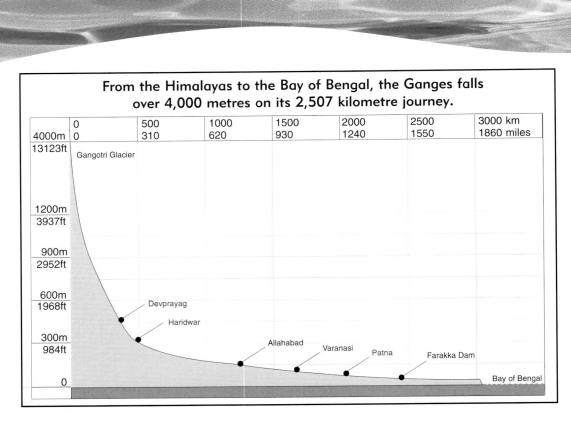

| | 0 | 500 | 1000 | 1500 | 2000 | 2500 | 3000 km |
| 4000m | 0 | 310 | 620 | 930 | 1240 | 1550 | 1860 miles |

From the Himalayas to the Bay of Bengal, the Ganges falls over 4,000 metres on its 2,507 kilometre journey.

13123ft — Gangotri Glacier

1200m / 3937ft

900m / 2952ft

600m / 1968ft — Devprayag

Haridwar

300m / 984ft — Allahabad — Varanasi — Patna — Farakka Dam

0 — Bay of Bengal

Further Information

USEFUL WEBSITES

http://templenet.com/Ganga/ganga.html
A site that gives information about the myths, legends and spiritual places along the Ganges River. You can also find out more about other important Indian sites using this web site.

http://www.factmonster.com/ce6/world/A0820149.html
Factmonster is an online information centre. This address will take you directly to the Ganges River entry, but use the search function to find additional information on 'India' or 'Bangladesh' for example.

http://library.thinkquest.org/22659/page2.htm
This takes you on an online tour down the Ganges River and will help you to learn more about the sites of interest and people living along the river's banks.

http://www.virtualbangladesh.com/bd_tour.html
An informative and interesting site which takes you on a virtual tour of Bangladesh. You will learn more about the country in general, and in particular more about the people, their lifestyles and culture.

BOOKS

Great Rivers: The Ganges by Michael Pollard (Evans Brothers, 2003)

The World's Rivers: The Ganges by D. Rogers, et al (Wayland, 1996)

Holy Places: The Ganges by Victoria Parker (Heinemann Library, 2004)

World in Focus: India by A. Brownlie Bojang and N. Barber (Wayland, 2006)

Economically Developing Countries: India by David Cummings (Wayland, 2000)

Themes in Geography: Rivers by Fred Martyn (Heinemann Library, 1996)

Earth Alert! Rivers by Shelagh Whiting (Wayland, 2001)

Glossary

Aqueduct A bridge that carries a canal.

Bank The side of a river.

Barrage A bridge across a river that holds or diverts water

Canal An artificial water channel for navigation or irrigation.

Channel The passage through which a river flows.

Cholera A disease of the gut.

Confluence The place where two rivers meet.

Current The flow of water in a certain direction.

Cyclone Tropical storms with very strong winds and heavy rains.

Dam A barrier that holds or diverts water.

Delta A geographical feature at the mouth of a river, formed by the buildup of sediment.

Diarrhoea A bacterial infection of the gut.

Distributary A branch of a river that carries water away from the main channel

Doab The land between the Ganges and the Yamuna rivers.

Drainage basin The area of land drained by a river and its tributaries.

Erosion The wearing away of land by natural forces.

Extinct A species which no longer exists.

Famine A long-term shortage of food.

Flood When a river spills its banks into land that is usually dry.

Ghats Stepped embankments on the edge of a river, used for prayers and bathing

Glacier A mass of snow and ice.

Global warming The gradual warming of the earth's atmosphere.

Habitat The home of animals and plants.

Headwater Water at the source of a river.

Herbicides Chemicals used to kill weeds.

Hydroelectric power (H.E.P.) Electricity generated by water as it passes through turbines.

Intercropping A system of growing several crops together so that each one benefits the others.

Jute An Asian plant. The rough bark is used to make rope, sacking and mats.

Meltwater Water produced by the melting of snow and ice.

Monsoon Seasonal rains caused by changes in the wind direction over south-east Asia.

Mutiny A rebellion, especially one in an army.

Nirvana A state of spiritual freedom, achieved by Hindus and Buddhists through meditation.

Partition A division into separate parts. British-controlled India was partitioned into India, Pakistan and East Pakistan (now Bangladesh) in 1947.

Pastoral A community or group of people who graze animals for their living.

Pesticides Chemicals used to kill insects and pests.

Pilgrims People who travel to visit holy places.

Population density The number of people living in a given area.

Pulses Edible seeds such as beans, peas and lentils. Pulses are an excellent source of protein and are eaten in large quantities by vegetarians.

Rapids Fast-moving stretches of water

Rotation farming Fields planted with different crops in alternate seasons.

Sal Large, valuable trees native to northern India.

Sediment Fine sand and earth that is moved and left by water, wind or ice.

Staple crops Foods that form the basis of the diet of an area. In India rice is the staple crop.

Subsistence farming Farming that provides food mainly for the farmer's household.

Terraced farming A system of growing crops on horizontal steps cut into a hillside.

Tributary A stream or river which flows into another larger stream or river.

Tubewell A well dug or drilled to reach deep water resources, and lined with a pipe or tube.

Typhoid A disease caused by contaminated food or water.

Watershed The boundary between two river basins

Wetland Area of marsh or swamp where the soil is saturated with water like a sponge.

Yield The total amount of crops grown in a measured area (normally a hectare) per year.

Index